Lead Generation for Professional Service Firms

Proven Marketing Strategies to Double Your Business

By David Smit

Do you need this book?

If you want to learn how to turn your website into your top lead generator, you need this book. As a financial advisor, you know the importance of using a targeted approach in securing your financial future – this book was developed specifically for financial advisors. It has all you need to know about:

- How to optimize your site so that the web drives traffic to you automatically;
- The only lead generation action plan that you will need;
- The top proven lead generation strategies and tips that will have your site working for you in no time flat.

Author

David Smit founded and currently heads up ResultsPoint –
ResultsPoint works hand in hand with Financial Planners
to develop business development strategies produces
results. David Smit's email address is:
david@resultspoint.com

Contents

<u>The Foundation</u> – Getting the basics right is the difference between an effective, lead generating website and one that is a waste of time

<u>The Process</u> - Getting more traffic is only the first step – you need a solid strategy to convert them in sales opportunities.

<u>Lead Gen in Action</u> – In this section you will learn how to get the leads flowing.

<u>The Next Steps</u>

The Foundation - What is a Lead…Really?

Leads are the bread and butter of a financial advisor's business. It thus makes sense to convert your website into a lead generator and online marketing machine – after all, the site will work even when you do not, making it easier for you to concentrate on your clients. This allows you to work on your business and not in your business.

It is vital, however, that you know in your own mind what a lead actually is.

Lead: /leed/ a lead, as it is used in the context of this book can be classified as a possible sales opportunity; someone who has shown some sort of interest in what it is your business can do for them.

In layman's terms, this is a point of contact with someone who is amenable to hearing more about your business and who is willing to give you the opportunity to tell them more about what you do.

A lead is NOT a guaranteed sale – all that can be guaranteed is that they are looking for information. You cannot rest on your laurels and expect the sale to fall in your lap; you will still have to earn it. However, having gotten the person in question to this point is pretty good progress – you have a foot in the door and the opportunity to tailor-make a solution for them.

Now that we understand what a lead is and is not, it is time to examine why it is important to start generating leads online and why your business may fail if you do not.

Why Generate Leads Online?

Some recent research ResultsPoint conducted showed 98% of financial advisors rely leads through word of mouth referrals. This is probably not going to surprise you in the least.

What may be of more interest, however, is that around about 41% of the respondents admitted to relying on cold calling in order to drum up new sales. Doesn't it make a lot more sense to get the clients to come looking for you instead of having to chase them?

With the help of this book, and a little effort on your part, you can make your online marketing do all the work instead and never have to face another cold call again. Follow the advice laid out here and you will soon find that you have a steady stream of leads coming in, with little effort from your side.

Personal referrals are the gold standard when it comes to lead referrals, especially when it comes to personal finance. People want to feel comfortable with the advisor and a personal referral is a great help with this. People are, however, also likely to want to satisfy themselves that this referral is right for them.

That is why it is imperative to have a solid online presence. Think of it this way – you move to a new city. You now need to start looking around for a new family doctor, accountant, etc. You ask your new colleagues and acquaintances for advice and get given a few names to choose from.

What is your next step? Do you just go to the first one recommended and hope for the best? If you are like most people, you will research the options online. A quick Google search will bring up most of the information you need to make an informed decision without you even setting foot out of the house.

One of my clients recently told me that he spoke to a lead that was referred to him, but the person didn't want to do business with them, because they could not find them online.

What this means for the professional is that clients will make split second decisions about whether or not to deal with you simply from what they see on the web – your snazzy office or top class receptionist won't even come into it if you have not done your due diligence with your online presence.

Studies have shown that around about 90% of people today will rather conduct a search online then pick up the phone. Let's face it; it is a lot simpler to do so. That means that you could be missing out on as much as 90% of the business out there simply because you do not have a website.

Action Step: Go online now and search for your name and your company name. What results do you get? Be objective – if you were a person looking for a financial advisor, would you be suitably impressed? Would you want to deal with the person or firm concerned? Is your website actively helping you to get leads?

The Foundation - Every Lead Generating Marketing Portal starts With a Solid Web Strategy

If you want to get the right sort of leads, you need to target your approach to your ideal target market. A simple way of looking at it is that you do not want to attract people who want to buy apples if you sell only pears.

By the same token, a targeted approach when setting up your online presence will ensure that it generates the right kind of leads. You need to ensure that the site is visible and attractive to your ideal client.

If you hope to get people to send in their personal details, you are going to need to develop a Marketing Portal that engenders a feeling of trust with the visitor. Your site needs to look professional and needs to work flawlessly. People should feel good after visiting your site.

The good news is that this is not such a difficult prospect. Sites that are successful at driving business tend to do the following simply and flawlessly:

1. Easy to find
2. Easy to navigate
3. Easy to use

1. Easy to Find

Of course, it is not much good having the best looking website in the world if no one can find it. You need to convince the major search engines that your site is a credible source of information. Your first step is to get traffic flowing to your site organically.

It is best to consider Search Engine Optimization from the outset when developing your website. Everything from the domain name to the content of the site is important here. SEO is about helping the people who are looking for your services to find your website.

It also means approaching the problem from different angles. Some people are going to know the name of your business, but what about those who do not? You also want to make sure that your site shows up near the top of the page in the more generic searches, like "Financial advisor in Melbourne", etc. Remember also that most people will not look beyond the first three or four sites listed in the results – still think optimization is something you can ignore?

2. Easy to Navigate

It is a fact that most web surfers will decide in 15 seconds or less whether or not your site is worth staying on. That is a very short window of opportunity and means that you have to spend some time on developing a landing page and navigation system that is easy to understand. If the information needed is not readily available, most people will simply click out and never come back.

There are two basic categories when it comes to the traffic to your site – prospects and existing clients. In each case, different information is going to be sought after.
Have a look at your site and objectively ascertain whether or not the site is simple to use for both groups:

- Is the navigation bar in the same place on each page?
- Are the titles easy to read and understand?
- Does your website follow the "3-click rule"?
  This means that your visitors can move to any page on the site in 3 clicks or less - The easier the better with this one.

3. Easy to Use

Steve Krug, a leading expert in the field of web usability, laid it out in simple terms in his book, "Don't Make Me Think." The basic message of the book was that, to be successful, a website had to be simple to use.

He also highlighted the importance of proper planning of the site in terms of the end user's experience on it. A simple site that is dead simple to use will always win out over even the flashiest site that requires some effort on the user's part. Here are some of the salient points that Krug identified when it comes to creating a website that works:

- Make the call to action unambiguous and ensure that it pertains to the content on hand.
- Data should be east to scan – break it up into smaller chunks, use spacing, use sub-headings.
- Use imagery carefully – if you overdo it, the site will take ages to load. Also only use images that reinforce your message.
- Keep the design uncluttered.
- Ensure that the end product looks and feels organized.

The Process

Lead Generation is a 3 step process:

1. Identify the offer;
2. Ask visitors to take action;
3. Create the exchange.

1. Identify the Offer

As a general rule, visitors to your site will be okay with handing out contact details if they believe that it will benefit them.

This can be something as simple as a free e-book or something more complicated like an email course. Whatever you choose, be sure that it is something that your target audience would find appealing and that they can really use.

You need to spend some time looking at life from your target market's point of view – consider what information might be important to them. By determining the different client personas you intend to deal with, you can come up with the ideal offer.

What you need to focus on now is creating content that is useful to your visitors – we will discuss the actual lead generation tips in the last section of this book.

Expert tip: It is a good idea to run various different tests in order to see which type of information is most valued by your audience – live testing is easy – all you need to do is to vary your content offering on a monthly basis over a three to six month period. The difference in the number of leads generated ought to give you a good indication of the usefulness of content.

2. Ask Visitors to Take Action

Calls to Action are simply that: A phrase or button that gets the consumer to move to the next phase.

What is the next logical step? What do you want the client to do? That is up to you – whether it is for them to request further information, for them to set up a meeting or simply to subscribe to your newsletter, the choice is yours. If you want them to listen to the call to action, you need to ensure that it is clearly set out and that it is really easy for your potential client. If they have to look for the call to action, you have lost – they will not.

Remember, most visitors will expect a call to action (CTA). If you have done your job properly, it can be a great tool to really kick your website up a notch. It creates interactivity for your site and allows your visitors to interact with you in a very real way. The benefit to you is in the information that you can glean in this way.

3. Create the Exchange

To actually get your lead from the visitor, you will need to offer them something of value in return. (People will not give out their personal details unless they are getting something in return.) You will have to get them to complete a form or send them to a landing page.

A landing page is quite simply just a one page form that pops up when someone clicks on an advertisement or on the relevant search engine result. It is also referred to as a "lead capture page" or a "form page".

This is where the exchange of information is going to take place. Visitors give you their details and you then give them what you promised. This entire process can be automated so will not cause additional effort on your part.

Take this book, for example. Before downloading it, you were directed to a landing page. On this page you had to provide some personal information such as your name and email address.

It is best to keep this page easy to understand and uncluttered. You need to be careful not to make it onerous to complete – remember most web users are looking for easy solutions, not additional work to do.

Here are some other tips for your landing page:

Fun and Short

There are three basic components to any good landing page – an appealing graphic, a short overview of what is on offer and a form to complete. Make sure that the graphic is light and fun but also that it fits in with the call to action (CTA) and the offer. Will the graphic appeal to your target clients?

Be Consistent

You do need to be truthful here – hyperbole will lead to your clients being felt let down and will have a negative impact on your business. Follow through with what you promised in your call to action (CTA). Consider even using similar wording. Follow through with the theme of your call to action (CTA) onto the landing page.

Remove Navigation

You can help to keep customers locked into the page by getting rid of the navigation bars – that way; they cannot easily just click to a different page when they realize that this is a lead generation form. The only button you want on this page is the "Submit" button. That way, people are more likely to spend time looking at what is on the page.

Expert Tip: Don't get greedy – ask for only as much data as you absolutely have to have. If people are confronted with a long form, they will think twice when it comes to completing it. People do not want to hand out every detail of their lives. Stick to the basics – Name, Telephone Number, Email Address and possibly City or Town. Be very careful about asking for anything else.

Lead Generation in Action - 6 Tried and Tested Lead Generation Tactics

1. Event Management

Hosting an event in order to touch base with existing clients, meet new clients and to network is a tried and tested way to boost business. If you want to cut down on the admin, you can run everything from the advertising of the event to the management of RSVPs on your website.

Another hot trend is to host a webinar – clients can connect with you without leaving their homes or offices. Webinars help you to reinforce your expertise and offer your clients a value add at a very reasonable cost to yourself. It can be likened to a content marketing exercise.

You get to steer the conversation, provide tips and highlight resources and also answer live questions. This gives you a great chance to build up a rapport with your clients and also helps to set you up as an expert in your field, increasing the trust that clients have in you.

A webinar is simple – people wishing to "attend" need to fill in their details in order to register. You will then know how many people to expect and what range of questions might come up. You can choose a niche topic to explore or can offer a more generalized webinar.

The big advantage of the webinar is that you are able to swell your email lists for future marketing exercises.

Webinars have been proven to have the highest conversion rates when it comes to marketing as the attendees are already interested in the topic being discussed and due to the interactive format of the event. It is a lot easier to convince someone to buy something from you when they can see you as a real person and not just some words on paper.

Expert Tip: Like any networking event, the success will depend on how well it is promoted. Send out teasers in your newsletter, make use of social media and don't forget to promote it via your website and blog as well.

2. Blog

It has long been established that a blog is a great tool when it comes to picking up leads. The basic reasons why this is so are:

1. ***Fresh Content*** – People want new and interesting content. Search engines are always looking for the most up to date information. Blogs allow the easy addition of new information and make lead generation that much easier.

   Maintaining fresh content is also vital in maintaining your page rank. Time and time again, websites that have a linked blog outperform those that do not.

   For the advisor that means that blogging is an essential tool to help direct potential clients to you.

   Blogging fleshes out your website and is easy to amend. It is a lot easier to fiddle with the content of a blog than it is with a website. Consistently adding quality content will also score big points with the search engines.

   The better you do with the search engines, the more organic traffic you can expect. You can quickly establish your blog and website as a credible source of information and will be able to maintain your search engine ranking.

To further increase the Search Engine Optimization (SEO) effectiveness, you need to judiciously use long tailed keywords in your post. (Think about search terms potential clients would use and include these naturally in each post – swapping them out regularly.)

2. *Establish Credibility* – You may be the most highly qualified financial advisor in the country but you still need to convince potential clients of this. The best way to do this is by maintaining a blog. This way you can connect and interact with clients and set yourself up as an expert at the same time. A well run blog will go a long way to building long-term relationships with clients.

3. *Provide Value* – Very few people are interested in hard sell techniques – blogs offer an alternative. The idea here is to inform your clients without trying to push sales down their throats. What you should aim to do is to get them thinking about the issue. If they feel that you are there for them and care more about them than a sale, they will come to you when

the time is right. The trust built in this manner can lead to a life-long relationship. Aim to deal with issues that come up time and time again. Or time blog posts to coincide with relevant world events.

3. Social Media

The big three in the social media game are Twitter, Facebook and LinkedIn. Twitter is great for sending short messages; Facebook is great for personal ones. For professionals, however, LinkedIn is the one to spend the most time on. The rules in LinkedIn are a lot stricter and rather than being a purely social application, it focuses on building professional relationships.

For the financial advisor, LinkedIn can be a goldmine – not only do you get to highlight your skills, you can build up a valuable database as well. LinkedIn, unlike any other social network, is a powerful business tool.

LinkedIn is a great way to show off your resume and gain credibility. Not only do you get to list your qualifications but you can also ask people you know to rate your skills as well. These online references can be a great way to establish yourself as an expert.

What you do need to do is to ensure that your profile is a proper reflection of who you are. This is not the place to be a shrinking violet – you need to bang your own drum here.

People want to deal with people who they feel they have something in common with or who they can get along with. Add just enough personal information to make you appear more like a real person.

Use LinkedIn to Generate Leads

Once you have set up your profile and have developed a good base of contacts, you can move on to bringing in new business. By developing target adverts, you are able to really boost your business in a way that traditional marketing methods are not able to.

> *Three tips for creating your LinkedIn ads:*
> 1. Set a budget
> 2. Craft a compelling ad that invites the user to learn more
> 3. Collect the leads for you or your sales team to follow up with

You can even set up a free consultation to review your website with a website consultant.

4. E-Book & White Papers

There is no way to overemphasize how imperative it is to give value when developing content. There is a lot of rubbish out there and web consumers are even more sophisticated than ever before. They want information, not a full on sales pitch. By providing content that is valuable, you are ensuring that they will return time and time again and that they will refer their friends as well. You get great exposure for your name and will be able to get top quality new business as well.

When it comes to information gathering, white papers and online brochures rank amongst the most important tools you can use. Keep them short and sweet and relevant and you will have a winner.

What you can do is to link this information to your landing page and a strong call to action. That way, people will need to give you their details in order to get the info they are looking for.

5. Videos

Content marketing is one of the top methods of online marketing – studies show that it engages your potential clients in a way that traditional marketing campaigns cannot achieve and that it can lead to as much as three times the number of leads.

Blogging is great, video is better. Online trends indicate that video blogs as opposed to simple text based blogs are a lot more effective in getting buy in from your audience. Where a picture paints a thousand words, a video can paint millions. It is said that a simple sixty second video is the equivalent of nearly two million words. It has also been proven that an average of 65% of people will carry on to your website after watching a video.

You do, however, need to choose the content carefully. You want to provide information that is useful. Consider the kind of information that your target market would want answered and work around that. Here are some ideas on how to choose content:

> **1. Answer FAQs** – Start by drawing up a list of questions that clients have asked and identify those that come up most often or those that deal with a current hot topic of discussion. All you really need is a short video – two or three minutes is ideal – select a question and provide a useful explanation.

This will not only provide value to your audience but also help to reinforce your own credibility as well.

2. Share Tips & Success Stories – Everyone wants to know how to look after their money, how to save for life events, etc. They love this information best when it is free. Choose one aspect, say saving for retirement for example, and run with that. A short, informative video will peak their interest enough for them to take a look at your website.

3. Interview People – You do not always need to be the star of the show. It can be interesting to get another perspective from a colleague. All you really need to do is to set up a short list of open-ended questions and then sit back and let your quest do most of the talking.

Whatever way you choose your ideas, be sure that the content is interesting and valuable to your target audience. If it helps them solve some sort of problem, you will be the winner. This is not the time for that sales pitch!

The fact is that short and sweet is the best way forward. By and large, viewers will only watch for a short time anyway so stick to three minutes at most to avoid the video becoming boring.

6. Personalized Content

To be successful at online marketing, you need to create the ideal customer experience. It is said that there is nothing as sweet to a person as the sound of their own name and this is a good concept to keep in mind when offering content. The trend towards offering a more personalized experience is gaining momentum, especially in the financial arena.

There are several ways to do this – offer surveys, etc. to help you understand who you are dealing with better. On the other hand, you could also make use of technology to really optimize your chances of lead generation. Not sure how?

The Next Step - Resources to Nurture Leads Online and More towards Closing the Deal

What to do next? Once the lead collection has begun, you will need to come up with a winning strategy.

In marketing terms this is referred to as nurturing. What this actually means is that you need to consistently communicate with your client and provide added value in order to grow the relationship.

Whether you want to call them directly or want to automate the entire process, nurturing these leads is a vital part of the plan.

Resources

- Hubspot's Lead Nurturing Guide
- 12-step Program for Lead Nurturing
- Lead Nurturing Best Practices Checklist

Want to learn more about ResultsPoint?

We work exclusively with financial advisors to build a strong, results-driven website. Our award-winning technology and outstanding, support, make us an industry favorite. Visit http://resultspoint.com for more details.

www.ingramcontent.com/pod-product-compliance
Lightning Source LLC
Chambersburg PA
CBHW051419170526

45165CB00004BA/1886